JENNY MYERS

COOK
ICT

A COLLECTION OF RECIPES FROM SOME OF WICHITA'S
MOST NOTABLE CHEFS AND RESTAURANTS

COOK
ICT

CONTENTS

INTRODUCTION 9

APPETIZERS 11

MAIN DISHES 29

DESSERTS 91

DRINKS & COCKTAILS 111

RESTAURANT LIST 137

A NOTE FROM THE AUTHOR 139

ACKNOWLEDGEMENTS 141

ABOUT THE AUTHOR 143

INTRODUCTION

Before families, friends, and community can gather to eat, someone must prepare the meal. That person designs a recipe, crafts the ingredients, and presents the meal with passion, love, and heartfelt excitement. That's what this book is about.

The food scene in Wichita is an eclectic mix of Midwestern practicality and coastal creativity, mingling flavors that range from the spice of Mexico to the earthy heat of the Middle East to the freshness of Vietnam. My husband and I love food, especially the food at local restaurants. Every recipe begins in the mind of a creative chef before it becomes a reality on our plates. There's an artistry, a story, behind every dish, and I like the idea of sharing that story.

Wichita chefs possess a contagious passion for food. Their humility, kindness, and love overwhelmed me as I spoke to each one of them. I knew these people were talented at their jobs (my tongue has told me that many times over!), but in hearing their stories, I didn't expect their love and excitement to spill over into my own life. I'm grateful for their hospitality. I have been blessed by the warmth of Wichita's chefs and restaurant owners, and I got a taste for their extraordinary determination to share their passions with ICT. Through this cookbook, I hope you will too.

APPETIZERS

NASHVILLE HOT CHICKEN WINGS   13

HAVARTI NACHOS   15

DATES MIGNON   17

HILL CRAB CAKES   20

SMOKED SALMON INVOLTINI   22

BUTTERNUT SQUASH BRUSCHETTA   23

SUMMER ROLLS   24

AVOCADO TOAST WITH
KING CRAB & CITRUS   27

NASHVILLE HOT CHICKEN WINGS

CHEF MIKE CASTANEDA   BADE TRUCK

Adding a bit of salt and pepper to the freshly fried wings will help it to stick to the wing itself, then the sauce will add a nice bit of flavor as well. When I was in Nashville cooking for Traeger Grills, I fell in love with the hot chicken wing. First thing I did was come home and make my own variation of it. It's different than what they do, but it's tasty! -Mike Castaneda

4-6 SERVINGS

1 lb chicken wings (broken down)
salt and pepper

SAUCE
4 oz garlic chile sauce
¼ cup brown sugar
2 tbls rice wine vinegar
salt and fresh cracked black pepper to taste

To make the sauce, mix together garlic chile sauce, brown sugar, and vinegar. Season with salt and pepper to taste.

Fry the chicken wings at 350 degrees for around 10 minutes or until done. Season with a pinch of salt and pepper while they are still hot out of the fryer.

Place the wings in a bowl and combine with sauce. Mix to coat.

For an extra touch, I blend sour cream with a small handful of cilantro and a small dash of apple cider vinegar as a dipping sauce to help with the heat of the wings.

HAVARTI NACHOS

CHEF ADRIAN DELODDER   BELLA VITA BISTRO

4 SERVINGS

white corn tortillas

HAVARTI CHEESE SAUCE
¼ cup butter
3 tbls flour
2 cups heavy cream
1 ½ cup Havarti cheese
1 cup andouille sausage, diced

BLACK BEAN SALSA
2 whole jalepenos, diced
1 cup black beans, drained
½ cup cannellini beans, drained
¼ cup green bell pepper, diced
¼ cup white onions, diced
4 oz cilantro, chopped
1 whole lime, juiced
½ cup tomatoes, diced
salt and pepper to taste

sour cream, for garnish

To make the tortilla chips, cut tortillas into 6 triangle shapes. Heat fryer to 325 degrees and cook chips until golden brown. Place chips on paper towel and lightly salt.

To make the cheese sauce, in a medium pot, melt the butter over medium high heat. Add the flour, and mix together with melted butter to make a roux. Add the heavy cream, and heat the mixture to a light simmer. Add the Havarti cheese and the sausage. Stir well until a creamy texture is achieved. Keep on a warm on low heat.

For the black bean salsa, mix all salsa ingredients together in a mixing bowl. Add salt and pepper to taste. Set aside.

To assemble the nachos, put the tortilla chips on a large serving plate, piled high. Drizzle the cheese sauce all over the chips, followed by spoonfulls of salsa on top of the chips. Put the sour cream in a squirt bottle. Squeeze, making long strides back and forth over the entire platter.

DATES MIGNON

CHEF JASON FEBRES TASTE AND SEE

*This recipe was inspired by my fascination for sweet and salty together.
It is my best selling tapa ever, plus, it's almost like candy! And come on, it has bacon! -Jason Febres*

50 SERVINGS

8 oz goat cheese
8 oz cream cheese
½ cup dried cranberries
½ cup green onions, chopped
50 medjool dates
25 bacon slices, cut in half

BALSAMIC REDUCTION
1 cup balsamic vinegar
1 cup sugar

arugula, for garnish
toothpicks, for assembly

To make the balsamic reduction, mix the balsamic vinegar and sugar in a medium sauce pot. Bring the mixture to a boil. Reduce the heat and simmer the mixture until it covers the back of a spoon. The reduction will thicken as it cools.

With a paring knife or using your fingers, split the dates on one side and remove the seed.

In a bowl, mix the goat cheese, cream cheese, cranberries, and green onions. Using a teaspoon, generously fill each date and wrap with a bacon strip. Secure with a toothpick.

Heat oil in a fryer to 350 degrees and fry dates until golden.

Assemble a bed of arugula on a platter. Place dates on top of the arugula and drizzle balsamic reduction on top.
Pair with a good Malbec.

"I love exposing people to the stuff they have never eaten before, and the best part is to see their facial expressions after they have tried it." -Chef Jason Febres

HILL CRAB CAKES

BRAD STEVEN   THE HILL

2-4 SERVINGS

1 lb crab meat
1 egg
1 tsp kosher salt
1 tsp freshly cracked black pepper
½ cup panko bread crumbs
½ small white onion, finely diced
½ green bell pepper, finely diced
½ red bell pepper, finely diced

EGG WASH
2 eggs
1 cup whole milk

Sauté onion, green pepper, and red pepper with 1 tablespoon of butter. Do not brown. Season with a pinch of salt and pepper. Pat dry with paper towels to remove excess moisture. Cool.

To make the egg wash, whisk together eggs and milk. Set aside.

Add all crab cake ingredients into a large mixing bowl. Combine together and refrigerate for 1 hour.

Preheat oven to 375 degrees.

Weigh out 2 ounce portions and form cakes with a 2 inch ring mold. Ensure the mixture combines by applying liberal pressure. Gently remove from ring mold and coat with egg wash. Immediately transfer to a bowl of panko bread crumbs and coat evenly.

Lightly pan fry crab cakes in oil on medium low heat. When one side is browned, flip the crab cakes. Transfer the pan to a 375 degree oven for approximately 10 minutes, or until the internal temperature reaches 140 degrees.

Serve with your choice of dipping sauces.

SMOKED SALMON INVOLTINI

CHEF JASON FEBRES   TASTE AND SEE

Involtini means "little bundles" in Italian. I LOVE small bites/tapas. These little guys look beautiful and are full of flavor. They have the fresh and tropical flavors from back home, Venezuela! -Jason Febres

24 SERVINGS

8-12 oz smoked salmon (pre-sliced)
4 oz cream cheese
1 large mango
2 avocados
1 bunch of cilantro
9 limes or key limes
multigrain crackers, or crackers of your choice

Portion the cream cheese in 24 pieces. Shape each into the form of a long roll or Crayon.

Split the avocados, working to get 24 even slices. Peel the mango and cut into 24 thin slices. Obtain 24 small sprigs of cilantro.

Place the salmon on a cutting board, enough for 24 pieces. Place 1 piece of each of the following onto salmon- cream cheese, mango, avocado, and cilantro. Roll each piece.

Cut the limes into quarters. Place each salmon involtini on a wooden tray or a stone slab. Decorate with the lime quarters and the crackers. Serve.

BUTTERNUT SQUASH BRUSCHETTA

CHEF BOBBY LANE   CHESTER'S CHOPHOUSE

*I like this recipe because it is fall/winter in every bite. You can change any or all ingredients.
It is very adaptable for varied tastes.- Bobby Lane*

15-20 SERVINGS

1 large butternut squash, peeled and diced small
2 shallots, chopped
¼ cup olive oil
salt and pepper to taste
1 cup sun-dried cranberries, chopped
1 cup crumbled blue cheese
2 sprigs fresh rosemary, chopped
1 baguette, sliced diagonally

Toss diced shallots and squash with olive oil and season with salt and pepper. Roast in a 350 degree oven until the squash is tender. Remove from oven and let cool.

Place cooled squash in a bowl. Add remaining ingredients, mix, and re-season if necessary.

Serve over toasted baguette.

SUMMER ROLLS

DUNG NGUYEN   PHO SPECIAL

We like this recipe because it is easy to prepare and fun for everyone to eat. Many times, we prepare all the vegetables and sauce, and cook the meat on a hot plate. Everyone can pick which meat and veggies they like and roll their own. -Dung Nguyen

2+ SERVINGS

boiled shrimp (desired amount)
steamed pork (desired amount)
1 cup lettuce, shredded
1 cup vermicelli rice noodles, cooked
rice paper
fresh mint leaves
cucumber, julienned
carrot, julienned
cilantro
jalepeno, thinly sliced

PEANUT SAUCE
3 cups water
half can of Coco Rico soda
½ cup peanut butter
1 cup hoisin
cornstarch
crushed peanuts

For the peanut sauce, bring water to a boil. Add Coco Rico soda, peanut butter, and hoisin sauce. Simmer on low heat for about 8-12 minutes. Stir and add cornstarch to desired viscosity. Add crushed peanuts on top.

To assemble the rolls, place all desired ingredients into prepared rice paper. Wrap up into a roll.

Serve with peanut dipping sauce.

AVOCADO TOAST WITH KING CRAB & CITRUS

CHEF BOBBY LANE   CHESTER'S CHOPHOUSE

16 SLICES

4 avocados, rough chopped
1 lime, juiced and zested
1 tsp Tabasco
1 tbls fresh cilantro, chopped
14" French baguette, sliced diagonally into 2" wide croutons
16 oz shredded Alaskan king crab
1 orange, juiced and zested
2 tbls olive oil
1 tbls chives, chopped
2 oranges, skinned and segmented
2 red breakfast radishes, diced
16 picked cilantro leaves
salt and pepper to taste

Pre-heat broiler in oven.

Drizzle sliced baguettes with oil and season with salt and pepper. Lightly toast the croutons under the broiler.

In a bowl, mash the avocado with lime juice and zest, and season with tabasco, cilantro, salt and pepper.

In another bowl, season crabmeat with orange juice, zest, olive oil, and chives.

Spread avocado puree on toasted baguettes. Top with crabmeat, and garnish with segmented oranges, diced radishes and cilantro leaves.

*Shrimp or other crab meat may be substituted in this recipe

MAIN DISHES

COFFEE-CHILI CRUSTED STEAK	31	ROYAL CHICKEN QORMA (SHAHI)	63
FATTOUSH SALAD WITH CHICKEN BREAST	33	LENTIL SOUP, TWO WAYS	64, 65
KANSAS BBQ BEEF BENEDICT	36	SLOW BRAISED BARBACOA WITH PICKLED RED ONIONS	66
SMOKED CHICKEN CATTIATORE	37	BAT OUT OF HELL MEATLOAF	69
PRAIRIE BISON SLIDERS	38	CHILES EN NOGADA	72
SRIRACHA SMOKED CHICKEN	42	TWISTED LINGUINI	74
BEEF BULGOGI	43	HIPPIE PORRIDGE	77
FALL PUMPKIN BISQUE	46	SHRIMP WELLINGTON WITH CORAL SAUCE	80
PORK BELLY WAFFLE SLIDERS	47	HARVEY'S AWARD-WINNING REUBEN	81
TANDOORI CHICKEN	50	GINTARA SAIKYO- YAKI (BLACK COD MARINATED WITH SAIKYO MISO)	82
ECUADORIAN CHEESY POTATO SOUP WITH SPINACH & AVOCADO	52	OCEAN ON PRAIRIE	86
GUJEOLPAN	57	BOLOGNESE	88
APPLE, POTATO AND BRIE SOUP	58		
GUINNESS STEW	59		

COFFEE-CHILI CRUSTED STEAK

CHEF MIKE CASTANEDA BADE TRUCK

Ensuring your steak is properly seasoned will make sure it is full of flavor. I'd much rather have an over-seasoned steak than one that has no flavor. I wanted to create this steak as an homage to my heritage. Being a Latin man, I love big, bold flavors, and growing up in South Central Kansas, steak is a staple. Infusing amazing chiles with beef is so delicious- the coffee was just an added factor! -Mike Castaneda

2 SERVINGS

2 steaks of your choice
kosher salt
cracked black pepper

RUB
2 tbls favorite coffee (I used Deathwish)
1 tsp ground Piquin chile
2 tsp ground Guajillo chile
1 tsp ground Chile de Arbol
1 tsp brown sugar
1 ½ tsp kosher salt
½ tsp black pepper
pinch of dried oregano

Liberally season the steaks with salt and pepper. After the steaks are seasoned on both sides, mix the coffee, ground chiles, brown sugar, salt, pepper, and oregano into a small bowl, Dust the steaks all over, front to back.

Cook the steak to medium rare over a hot grill. Let steak rest for about 10 minutes before slicing.

Alternative cooking methods:
-Preheat oven to 500 degrees. Heat oil in a cast iron skillet. Sear the seasoned steaks in the skillet for 2 minutes per side. After searing, move skillet into the oven and cook steaks for 7-10 minutes. Top with melted butter.

-After seasoning steaks, place the steaks in a vacuum sealer machine and sous vide the steaks at 140 degrees for 90 minutes.

FATTOUSH SALAD
WITH GRILLED CHICKEN BREAST

CHEF JD HARVEY   THE CANDLE CLUB

The longer you marinate the chicken, the tastier it is!
Make sure to marinate for at least 8 hours for optimum flavor. -JD Harvey

4 SERVINGS

DRESSING
1 cup balsamic vinegar
2 cups light olive oil
1 tbls kosher salt
½ tbls ground sumac
1 medium red onion
1 medium red bell pepper
3-5 garlic cloves
¼ cup Dijon mustard

SALAD
4 chicken breasts
2 hearts of romaine lettuce
½ head of iceberg lettuce
1 cup feta cheese, diced
½ red onion, julienned
½ red pepper, diced
10 slices English cucumber
20 grape tomatoes
8 artichoke heart quarters
4 oz pita chips, crumbled
½ tbls powdered sumac

To make the dressing, cut the red onion into eigths and red bell pepper (seeds removed) into fourths, and place in a food processor with a chopping blade. Add all other dressing ingredients except oil and mustard. Purée until very smooth. Once ingredients are puréed, slowly add oil and mustard with machine running on low. Purée until emulsified. Once emulsified, continue to run processor for 3 minutes. Note: This dressing will separate when settled. Shake in container or use a wire whisk to bring back together. This makes about 1 quart- enough for marinating chicken and four salads.

Use 1 cup of dressing to marinate 4 boneless chicken breasts. Cover and refrigerate to marinate for at least 8 hours. Once marinated, fire up the grill and cook chicken to internal temperature of 165 degrees. After grilling, allow chicken to relax for 5 minutes, then slice thin to top salad.

Roughly chop hearts of romaine lettuce and iceberg lettuce. Add additional salad ingredients and toss together with remaining dressing to taste. Keep in mind a little bit goes a long way! Toss until everything is well coated. Plate salads and top with sliced chicken and garnish with powdered sumac.

"With over 20 years of culinary expertise, my goal was to create high quality comfort food in a fun and relaxing environment. Throughout the years, Wichitans have opened their hearts to my rendition of the modern Americana style cuisine. I love developing new restaurant concepts and menus that Wichitans will love and rave about for years to come. Wichita is a food passionate community with a fine appreciation for quality ingredients and creative food." -Chef JD Harvey

KANSAS BBQ BEEF BENEDICT

CHEF BOBBY LANE   CHESTER'S CHOPHOUSE

Everyone loves eggs Benny. The sweetness of the brisket and orange hollandaise is a great combo. -Bobby Lane

1 SERVING

1 Thomas English muffin
2 eggs
4 oz bbq beef brisket
3 oz orange hollandaise
crispy shallots (can use onion rings or onion straws)
sunflower sprouts (can use any local sprout, for color and crunch)

ORANGE HOLLANDAISE
4 egg yolks
8 oz melted clarified butter
1 orange, zested and juiced
Tabasco sauce
Worcestershire sauce
salt and pepper to taste

To prepare orange hollandaise, whisk yolks over a water bath until pale yellow and thickened. Remove from heat. Off heat, slowly pour the butter in a steady stream until incorporated. Add the orange zest and juice, a dash of Tabasco, and Worcestershire. Season with salt and pepper. Keep warm.

Crispy fry the shallots or onion rings.

Poach the eggs in salted water.

To assemble, toast English muffin and place warmed brisket on top, along with the poached egg. Cover with the orange hollandaise and garnish with sprouts and onions.

SMOKED CHICKEN CATTIATORE

CHEF JOHN CONKLIN

6-10 SERVINGS

2 cups apple wood chips, soaked in riesling wine for 1 hour
12 chicken thighs, deboned
12 strips thick-cut peppered bacon
12 toothpicks
4 cups soffrito (leeks, carrots, celery; 50/25/25)
2 cups bacon, rough chopped
1 cup sugar
2 cups red wine (preferably sangiovese or Tuscan)
2 cups red wine vinegar
2 cups chicken stock
2 lbs enoki mushrooms
25 Roma tomatoes, chunked
2 cups tomato juice
2 lb unsalted butter, divided
1 oz fresh marjoram, chopped
2 oz grated Parmesan cheese

Wrap chicken thighs tightly with bacon (you should only be using 1/2- 3/4 of each bacon strip). Use a toothpick to secure. Season with salt and pepper, and set aside to air dry.

In a large braising pot, melt 1/4 pound (1 stick) of butter and slowly sweat down soffrito mix with chopped bacon. Once the onions are translucent, turn to high heat, stirring frequently so bacon is crispy, but not burnt. Still on high heat, add sugar and thoroughly coat soffrito and bacon. Caramelize for five minutes, or until a deep brown color is attained on carrots and bacon. Deglaze with red wine and red wine vinegar. Add Roma tomatoes and reduce by half, stirring often to break down tomatoes. Set aside to cool.

In a skillet or cast iron pan(s), sear chicken thighs, rotating often to achieve a golden brown color on bacon. In glass baking dishes lay chicken thighs out flat and add soffrito and bacon mix over the top, filling in all spaces between the thighs. Slowly add 3/4 of sauce base to baking dishes and bake uncovered at 400 degrees for 30-45 minutes or until chicken thighs are cooked thoroughly. While thighs are baking, reduce the rest of the sauce base with the tomato juice at a medium heat, skimming fat line from the top. Reduce by half, and whisk in the rest of the butter until a sauce consistency is attained.

Whether serving as a platter or as individual portions, ladle out soffrito base first, using mostly vegetables. Top with chicken thighs, and finish with a "John Swoop" of buttery sauce. Top with marjoram, and grated Parmesan.

PRAIRIE BISON SLIDERS

TRAVIS & BROOKE RUSSELL, DREW THOMPSON   PUBLIC

When this recipe was introduced on our very first menu, we immediately knew that it would be the most popular item at our restaurant for years to come. Six months after opening Public, we were contacted by producers at the Travel Channel show "BBQ Crawl" hosted by BBQ champion Danielle Bennett. Our slider recipe was chosen to be featured on the show as the producers wanted to show off a recipe that used bison as the main protein. Years later, the episode is still airing on The Travel Channel, and we still get new customers who are driving through Kansas and stop by to try our Prairie Sliders. -Travis Russell

24 SLIDERS

2 lbs ground bison
1 lb ground beef (81%-19%)
¼ cup seasoning (recipe below)

6 slices cheddar cheese
24 slider buns

SLIDER SEASONING
¼ cup finely ground espresso
¼ cup ground dried porcini (or available) mushrooms
½ cup Montreal steak seasoning

ONION JAM
1 tbls unsalted butter
2 med onions
¼ cup sugar
⅓ cup dry red wine
⅓ cup grenadine
salt to taste

MUSTARD AIOLI
2 cups mayo
1/2 cup yellow mustard
1/2 cup whole grain mustard
2 tbls lemon juice

To prepare the onion jam, finely dice onions or chop in a food processor. Place onions and butter into a saucepan and sweat over medium heat 10-15 minutes. Add remaining ingredients and reduce on low heat until liquid is absorbed and consistency sticks to a spoon. Set aside to cool.

For the mustard aioli, add mustard and lemon juice to the mayo and stir well.

To make the sliders, combine ingredients in a large mixing bowl and massage seasoning into meat. Be careful not to mush the texture of the meat. (We utilize a mix of bison and beef in order to keep the patties from drying out while on the grill. The added beef fat is needed, as bison is often very lean.)

Use your pointer finger and thumb to create a round mold to form the meat into approximately 2 ounce patties that resemble little pucks and place on a pan or sheet tray lined with parchment paper.

Cook over medium heat and be careful not to cook too quickly as they will dry out. Several minutes on each side should suffice.

Add quartered slices of rich New York-style cheddar cheese and melt onto slider or cocktail buns. Consider choosing Vermont cheddar, or use challah or pretzel buns to mix up your style of slider.

"My dad taught me how to cook in our west Wichita home so it's very special to be working as a chef in Wichita. I learned new techniques and recipes while away in Lawrence and St. Louis, but I'm now surrounded by the recipes written by my family in Norwich and Medicine Lodge. Living in south central Kansas, we are lucky to be surrounded by farmers and vendors who are able to provide our restaurant with the ingredients we need to make beautiful and healthy dishes. We are proud to say that all of our proteins are produced in this region, our breads are baked in Wichita, our dairy is local, and we serve vegetables and fruit from a long list of local farms." -Travis Russell

SRIRACHA SMOKED CHICKEN

CEDRIC TAYLOR   DELANO BARBEQUE COMPANY

20 SERVINGS

20 pieces bone-in chicken
1 tsp seasoning salt
½ tsp sugar
½ tsp onion powder
3 tbls Sriracha
½ tsp paprika
1 lime, juiced

Rinse chicken in cold water. Place chicken pieces in a bowl and squeeze the lime juice over the chicken.

Mix all seasonings and spices together in a separate bowl. Add seasoning mixture to the chicken, coating the chicken thoroughly on all sides.

Cook chicken on a smoker for 2.5 hours at 225 degrees.

Serve hot.

BEEF BULGOGI

KERRY LEE   HOT STONE KOREAN GRILL

Korean dishes are not only delicious, but also beautiful. I want to spread the beauty of Korean dishes. -Kerry Lee

2 SERVINGS

1 lb beef sirloin or round steak
4 oz onions
2 oz carrots
2 oz green bell peppers
1 tbls chopped green onion, for garnish
sesame seeds, for garnish

SAUCE
½ tsp ground black pepper
5 tbls soy sauce
2 tbls yellow sugar
1 tbls honey
2 tbls ground garlic
2 tbls sesame oil

To make the sauce, place all sauce ingredients in a bowl and whisk to blend. Set aside.

Slice beef thinly against the grain and place the beef in a bowl. Pour the prepared sauce over the beef. Cover and refrigerate for at least 1 hour or overnight.

Cook the beef in a frying pan over high heat. When the meat starts to brown, add sliced onions, sliced carrots, sliced green bell peppers and cook until the meat is well done.

Decorate dish with green onions and sesame seeds on top of the bulgogi.

Serve with rice.

"Honesty is what connects us and customers, and I believe that can be done through the dishes we serve." -Kerry Lee

FALL PUMPKIN BISQUE

CHEF BOBBY LANE   CHESTER'S CHOPHOUSE

An easy, one pot soup that tastes great and makes the house smell like fall. Make lots, people love it! -Bobby Lane

8 SERVINGS

1 large pumpkin, peeled, deseeded, and diced
1 large onion, chopped
2 shallots, chopped
12 cups chicken stock
½ cup brown sugar
½ cup honey
1 tsp nutmeg
1 tsp cinnamon
salt and white pepper to taste

In a medium pot, heat 2 tablespoons of olive oil; add onions and shallots. Cook until transluscent. Add diced pumpkin and stock. Simmer 20-25 minutes until squash is very soft. Puree in small batches in a blender or food processor, and season with brown sugar, honey, and spices to taste. If soup is thick, add additional stock to thin it to desired consistency.

If desired, garnish soup with snipped chives, chopped walnuts, pistachio oil, or chopped lobster meat. You may also toast the pumpkin seeds to use for garnish.

PORK BELLY WAFFLE SLIDERS

CHEF BOBBY LANE   CHESTER'S CHOPHOUSE

4 SERVINGS

8- 2 oz pieces of braised pork belly
16 mini waffles
8 oz softened cream cheese
5 tbls maple syrup
4 oz fresh arugula
jalepeno red pepper jelly

JALEPENO RED PEPPER JELLY
2 ½ cups red bell peppers, finely chopped
1 ¼ cups green bell peppers, finely chopped
¼ cup jalepeno, finely chopped
1 cup apple cider vinegar
5 cups white sugar
1 ½ packages powdered pectin (2.63 total ounces)

Jalepeno jelly can be made 2-3 days in advance. To prepare the jalepeno jelly, bring peppers and vinegar to a boil. When boiling, add sugar. Bring back to a boil for one minute, then add pectin and remove from heat.

Combine softened cream cheese with 3 tablespoons of maple syrup and reserve.

Crisp pork belly in a skillet and drizzle with 3 tablespoons of maple syrup. Allow it to get nice and sticky.

Toast the mini waffles. To build the sliders, spread maple cream cheese and jalepeno jelly on waffle halves. Top with braised pork belly and arugula.

Note: Use additional jelly as a dipping sauce for the sliders to add an extra kick of heat.

"Wichitans are very adventurous eaters. They are willing to try new foods and combinations. We want Chester's Chophouse to be everyone's favorite restaurant. Whether that means a special occasion for some- for the fresh, ever-changing specials and wine choices, or being a more frequent stop for people that look beyond the higher priced items. We try to attain the highest levels of service and hospitality on a daily basis." -Bobby Lane

TANDOORI CHICKEN

SYED JILLANI   KABABS...

4 SERVINGS

2 lbs bone-in chicken pieces
½ cup tandoori spice
1 cup plain yogurt
½ cup oil
½ cup garlic, minced
¼ cup paprika

1 cucumber, sliced
1/2 onion, sliced
green pepper, sliced
red pepper, sliced

cilantro, for garnish
lemon, for garnish

Mix chicken together with tandoori spice, yogurt, oil, garlic, and paprika in one large bowl. Cover and refridgerate to marinate overnight.

Place chicken on a baking sheet and bake in oven for 20-25 minutes at 400 degrees.

Plate chicken with cucumber, onion, green pepper, and red pepper. Garnish with cilantro and lemon slices. Serve with rice or baked naan bread.

ECUADORIAN CHEESY POTATO SOUP WITH SPINACH AND AVOCADO

CHEF KELLY RAE LEFFEL, SARAH OSBORN-BENNETT   TANYA'S SOUP KITCHEN

This recipe is the perfect blend of all my favorite flavors. Not only is it delicious, it's a gorgeous soup, and the colors are bright and vibrant. A close friend of mine, who now works for us at TSK, told me stories of her family's recipes passed down from her great grandparents who are from Ecuador. Those stories are what inspired this recipe. -Kelly Rae Leffel

8 SERVINGS

2 tbls butter
1 onion, diced
2 garlic cloves, minced
2 tsp cumin
1 tsp paprika
½ tsp turmeric
2 lbs Yukon Gold potatoes, quartered
4-5 cups vegetable stock
2 cups heavy cream
8 oz cream cheese, at room temperature
1 cup queso fresco
1 bag fresh spinach, chopped
1 bunch cilantro, chopped
salt and pepper

1 lime, zested and juiced, for garnish
avocado, for garnish
queso fresco, for garnish
hot sauce (optional)

Melt butter in a pot and sauté onions and garlic with cumin, paprika, and turmeric. Add the rest of the ingredients except the spinach and cilantro. Bring pot to a boil and reduce heat to a simmer until the potatoes are cooked, about 30 minutes. Stir in spinach and cilantro right before serving.

Garnish with lime zest and juice, avocado, cheese, and hot sauce.

"I was born and raised in ICT. I tried living in other cities, but home is where the heart is. I did most of my growing up in the kitchen- dance parties with my mom, sharing laughs with close friends, and I've thought a lot about life over the stove. For me, cooking in Wichita is like being at home, my favorite place to be."

-Chef Kelly Rae

GUJEOLPAN

KERRY LEE   HOT STONE KOREAN GRILL

Gujeolpan is Emperor's cuisine with 9 deliciacies.
We have to ensure that nine delicacies are in a harmony and avoid any strong spices. -Kerry Lee

2 SERVINGS

1 pack of pickled radish
4 oz sliced beef sirloin
4 oz cooked shrimp
4 oz crab meat
4 oz cucumbers, julienned
4 oz shiitake mushrooms, julienned
4 oz carrots, julienned
2 eggs
soy sauce
salt and pepper
oil

SAUCE
2 tbls Korean mustard paste
1 tbls sugar
1 tbls vinegar
1 tbls lemon juice
pinch of salt

Whisk together all ingredients for sauce and set aside.

Cut the beef into strips. Cook the beef in heated oil in a fry pan with one teaspoon of soy sauce and a pinch of ground black pepper.

Cook mushrooms with a pinch of salt in oil in a fry pan. Repeat this step with carrots, crab meat, and shrimp.

Separate the egg yolks from the egg whites and place in separate bowls. Add a pinch of salt into each. Whisk, and cook separately with oil on low heat. Once the eggs are cooled, cut into strips.

Place the sweet and sour pickled radish in the middle of a large plate and arrange all other 8 ingredients around it. To assemble, use the radish as a wrap, and fill with desired ingredients.

APPLE, POTATO, AND BRIE SOUP

ALI YASSINE   COLLEGE HILL DELI

2-4 SERVINGS

2 tbls extra virgin olive oil
1 medium yellow onion, chopped
2 celery stalks, chopped
2 Yukon Gold potatoes, peeled and chopped
5 Lady Alice apples, peeled and chopped
4 cups chicken broth
3 oz Brie cheese, rind removed and chopped
½ tsp salt
½ tsp black pepper
2 tsp fresh thyme leaves

In a medium stock pot, heat oil over medium high heat. Add onion, celery, and potatoes and cook for 8-10 minutes, or until browned and tender. Add apples and cook another 3-5 minutes, or until tender. Add broth and raise temperature to bring to a boil. Boil for 1 minute, then reduce heat to medium and simmer for about 10 minutes, or until all ingredients are very tender. Whisk in the cheese, and add salt, pepper, and thyme.

GUINESS STEW

CHEF JOHN CONKLIN

A big shout to my family, and where my passion for food and the finer aspects of communing with loved ones comes from. -John Conklin

6-8 SERVINGS

4 cups yellow onion, rough chopped
2 cups celery, rough chopped
2 cups carrots, rough chopped (the carrots will need to be blanched, i.e half cooked)
4 tbls roasted garlic paste
2 tbls fresh thyme, picked
4 tbls fresh rosemary, chopped
2 tbls fresh marjoram
bouquet garni (6 sprigs rosemary, 12 sprigs thyme, 2 bay leaves, 5 sprigs marjoram, wrapped in cheese cloth)
7 large potatoes, poached and held to side
5 pounds leg of lamb, rough chopped, tossed with salt & pepper and 1 cup of Worcestershire sauce
10 cups veal stock
4 cups Guinness dark draft beer
1 medium red cabbage, shredded
½ cup red wine

In a large braising pan, with ¼ cup olive oil, sear onions, celery, carrots, and fresh chopped herbs with the roasted garlic paste. Stir constantly until the onions are semi-translucent.

Meanwhile, in a large boiling pot, heat veal stock, Guinness, and bouquet garni until a light simmer is attained. Using a strainer over the veal base, add vegetable mix to strainer and thoroughly drip dry so all residual liquid content goes into the stew base. Hold vegetables to the side. Using the same braising pan that was used for the vegetables, sear the lamb on high heat. The lamb should be golden brown on the outside, rare on the inside. Strain liquids into the veal base, using the same method as the vegetable mix. Set the lamb alongside the vegetables. Taste and check for flavor. Profile should have a savory, yet lightness once lamb and vegetables are thoroughly mixed.

Take the bouquet garni out of veal and Guinness base, and set to the side. Add the previously poached potatoes and bring to a simmer, stirring frequently, to ensure that potatoes don't stick to the bottom of the pot. Once potatoes are hot, use an immersion blender to puree potatoes into the base (this is your thickening agent for the stew base). If more potatoes are needed (use your judgement), a little extra boiled potato between the Irish is never a bad thing! Strain liquid through a fine mesh strainer and put it back into your boiling pot. The excess from the strainer can be tossed. Making sure that the consistency for the liquid base is thick, add all other ingredients to the base. Bring to a simmer for 10 minutes, stirring frequently. Set aside.

In a skillet or large saute pan, on high heat, add cabbage with ¼ stick of butter. Stir constantly. When the cabbage begins to sizzle and scorch, deglaze with red wine. Stir for 30-45 seconds and remove from heat. Pat dry cabbage thoroughly.

Ladle stew into bowls. Each bowl that is served should be topped with about 2 ounces of cabbage.

"I have no bigger love than that of the likes of Julia Child, Thomas Keller, and Daniel Boulud. They have been inspirations to push the boundaries of my own palate and what I view in the world of what true 'joy-gasmic' food is. Always remember that patience is a godly virtue of a true cook." -Chef John Conklin

ROYAL (SHAHI) CHICKEN QORMA

SYED ABBAS   ZAYTUN BISTRO

Chicken qorma has a rich and wonderful aromatic taste. It is made on very special occsions throughout India and Pakistan since Mughal ruled centuries ago. My mother always made this on special occasions. -Syed Abbas

4 SERVINGS

16 oz chicken breast
8 oz plain greek yogurt
8 oz heavy cream
1 stick salted butter
2 medium onions, sliced
1 inch fresh ginger root, chopped
2 cloves garlic, chopped
1 medium tomato, chopped
10-12 fresh curry leaves (available at Asian grocery stores)
1 tsp coriander
1 tsp cumin
½ tsp cayenne pepper
1 tsp turmeric
1 ½ tsp salt
2 black cardamom pods
10 green cardamom pods
10 cloves
2 small cinammon sticks
1 tsp black cumin
10 black peppercorns
10 blanched whole almonds
10 raisins

cilantro, for garnish

Melt butter on medium heat in a large pot. Add chicken, onions, ginger, and garlic. Cook until chicken is cooked half-way through.

Add yogurt, tomato, and all ground and whole spices. Add curry leaves, and cover the pan. Cook for at least 25 minutes or until chicken is cooked through. Add almonds, raisins, and heavy cream, and let it simmer for about 10 minutes. Add salt to taste.

Garnish with cilantro and serve with fluffy Basmati rice.

LENTIL SOUP

ALI KASSINE   COLLEGE HILL DELI

4 SERVINGS

2 cups brown lentils, rinsed
14 cups water
2 tsp salt
¼ cup long-grain rice
½ lb lean ground beef
1 tsp ground black pepper
3 tbls extra virgin olive oil
1 medium yellow onion, chopped
1 tbls cumin
½ cup fresh parsley, chopped
2 medium potatoes, peeled and diced

In a large pot over medium low heat, combine brown lentils, water, and 1 teaspoon of salt. Bring to a simmer and cook, stirring occasionally for 1 hour.

Remove pot from heat. Using a handheld immersion blender or food processor fitted with a chopping blade, blend lentils for 1-2 minutes or until smooth. If desired, strain the soup to remove any pulp from the lentil skins.

Set the pot over low heat. Add long-grain rice and cook, stirring occasionally for 10 minutes.

In a small bowl, combine ground beef, ½ teaspoon of salt, and ½ teaspoon of black pepper. Form mixture into approximately 25 (½ inch) meatballs. Place meatballs in a hot skillet, turning over every 2 minutes until browned on all sides and cooked through. Add cooked meatballs to soup.

In a small skillet, heat extra virgin olive oil. Add yellow onion and sauté for 5 minutes. Add sautéed onion to soup.

Add remaining ½ teaspoon of salt, ½ teaspoon of black pepper, cumin, parsley, and potatoes to the soup. Stir to combine. Cook for 5 minutes. Remove from heat and serve.

LENTIL AND SPLIT PEA SOUP

TONY ABDAYEM   LA GALETTE CAFE & DELI

4 SERVINGS

2 ¼ cup green and brown lentils
4 tbls olive oil
2 medium onions, finely chopped
1 ½ tsp ground cumin or cinnamon
½ tsp black pepper
salt or chicken base to taste
4 celery sticks, chopped
1 potato, chopped

Pick lentils clean of any impurities and place them in a large saucepan. Cover with water and place over high heat. Bring to a boil, and reduce heat to medium. Stir the lentils occasionally. Simmer for 45 minutes, or until tender.

Put the olive oil and chopped onion in a large pot. Sauté onions over medium heat until the onions become golden. Add the potatoes and celery, and cover with water. Bring to a boil and simmer for 15 minutes. When the potatoes and celery are tender, add pepper, cumin, and salt (or chicken base). Add the cooked lentils and peas. Serve hot.

SLOW BRAISED BARBACOA WITH PICKLED RED ONIONS

MICHAEL FARHA   DISTRICT TAQUERIA

4 SERVINGS

2 pounds beef brisket, trimmed
½ white onion, sliced thick
4 garlic cloves, smashed
1 tbls kosher salt
1 tbls black pepper
1 tbls chili powder
2 tbls granulated garlic
1 tbls granulated onion
1 tsp cumin
¼ tsp ground clove
3-4 cups Negra Modelo or dark lager
canola oil

PICKLED RED ONIONS
1 large red onion, cut in half and thinly sliced
2 garlic cloves, browned
2 cups white vinegar or apple cider vinegar
1 tbls sugar

guacamole or avocado slices
cotija cheese
lime wedges

Rub brisket with about 2 tablespoons of canola oil. Sear brisket over a hot grill or in a hot pan until a char is achieved. Place the brisket in an oven safe braising pot and add all ground spices, including salt and pepper. Rub ground ingredients all over the brisket. Add fresh onion and garlic cloves, and cover with about 1 cup of beer. Allow to set an hour or overnight in fridge. When ready to cook, add the rest of the beer until the brisket is just slightly covered. Put a lid on the pot, or cover tightly with foil. Cook in a 350 degree oven for about 3-4 hours. Take out and allow the meat to rest. Pull apart or shred the meat with forks.

To make the onions, dissolve the sugar in boiling vinegar. Once dissolved, pour the mixture over red onions. Cover and let cool to room temperature. Place in fridge to cool completely and to achieve the vibrant, neon red color.

Heat up your favorite tortillas, preferably locally made La Tradicion corn or flour! Place a dollop of homemade guacamole or avocado slices in the tortilla. Add a heaping mound of barbacoa, cotija cheese, and top with pickled red onions. Plate and serve with lime wedges.

BAT OUT OF HELL MEATLOAF

CHEF PATRICK & TIMIRIE SHIBLEY   DOO-DAH DINER

This is the first dish I made for Patrick when we started dating in 2009. He said, "This is the best meatloaf I've ever had, and if we ever open a restaurant, it must be on the menu!" My mother made this when I was growing up. I didn't like it because she used green bell pepper. When I substituted red pepper for the green, it changed the flavor profile. The most important ingredient in this recipe is love! Extra dashes if necessary. -Timirie Shibley

8 SERVINGS

2 lbs ground round beef
2 eggs, beaten
1 medium onion, chopped
1 medium red bell pepper, chopped
8 oz Cracker Barrel sharp cheddar cheese, cut to 1/4 inch cubes
2 slices thin cut jalepeno bacon, raw
1 cup Heinz Chili Sauce
½ cup bread crumbs
3 tbls worcestershire
½ tsp salt
½ tsp pepper

In a large bowl, mix all ingredients except bacon and chili sauce. It's best to mix by hand. Mold into a loaf shape and place in a baking dish. Place bacon on top of the loaf. Spread chili sauce on top of the bacon, and put in the oven to bake for 1 hour at 375 degrees.

Remove from baking dish, and put on a serving plate to slice.

"Cooking food in Wichita is special for us because it's our hometown! We often have the opportunity to cook for people that were instrumental in our lives growing up here- former teachers, coaches, ministers, etc." -Timirie Shibley

CHILES EN NOGADA

MARIO QUIROZ & MARA GARZA   MOLINO'S

*This is a typical dish from Puebla, Mexico. It is colorful and it has a full body of flavors.
Cook with patience. - Mara Garza*

8-10 SERVINGS

10 poblano peppers

2 ½ pounds Balltip or Sirloin steak
2 ½ pounds pork
3 tsp garlic powder
3 tsp salt
1 onion, chopped
3 tsp beef base
3 tsp paprika

NOGADA SAUCE
2 8 oz bars of cream cheese
2 cups milk
1 tsp cinnamon
1 tsp nutmeg
¼ cup sugar
1 oz butter

FRUIT MIXTURE
1 pear, chopped
1 peach, chopped
1 apple, chopped
½ cup sugar
½ cup raisins
½ cup almonds, chopped
½ cup pecans, chopped
4 tbls butter
1 tsp nutmeg
1 tsp cinnamon
6 oz white wine

cilantro, for garnish
pomegranate seeds, for garnish

Roast poblano peppers over a grill or under a broiler. Turn until all sides are blistered. Remove from the grill and place in a Ziplock bag. Allow to sweat and cool. After poblanos have cooled, remove the seeds and veins, and peel off the skin. Set aside.

Heat approximately 2 tablespoons of oil in a sauté pan. Place meat in the sauté pan, along with onions, garlic powder, beef base, salt, and paprika. Bring to simmer and cook for about 20 minutes.

To make the nogada sauce, blend all sauce ingredients except for the butter in a bowl. In a large saucepot, melt the butter. Add the blended sauce, and cook for 8 minutes on medium high heat until a thick consistency is achieved. Set aside, and keep warm.

Melt butter in a sauté pan over medium heat. Add all fruit ingredients and cook for approximtely 8 minutes. Reduce fruit mixture with white wine, and simmer for 8 minutes more.

When meat is ready, roughly chop and combine together with fruit mixture.

Slice an opening down the long side of the roasted poblanos. Fill the poblanos with the meat and fruit mixture. Place poblanos on serving plate, and pour nogada sauce on the top. Garnish with cilantro and pomegranate seeds.

TWISTED LINGUINI

BRAD STEVEN   WINE DIVE

2 SERVINGS

4 tsp pesto
2 cups zucchini and squash, chopped
½ cup cherry tomatoes, halved
½ cup mixed mushrooms, chopped
2 tsp Sriracha
2 tbls garlic and shallots, finely diced
salt and pepper to taste
12 oz linguini pasta
2 tbls olive oil

Cook pasta according to package directions. In a sauté pan, add 1 tablespoon of olive oil over medium heat. Add the garlic and shallots, and cook until translucent. Add the rest of the vegetables, and season with salt and pepper. Cook until the vegetables are slightly softened. Add strained linguini to the pan and mix in pesto and Sriracha. Serve.

HIPPIE PORRIDGE

CHAROLETT KNAPIC   BEAUTIFUL DAY CAFE

This is a great tasting, ready to eat breakfast or snack that is also good for your body. Don't add too much milk to the dry ingredients until thoroughly mixed, or there will be lumps of chia/flax. -Charolett Knapic

4 SERVINGS

2 cups oats
¼ cup flax/chia meal
1 tbls cinnamon
½ tsp salt
½ gallon vanilla almond milk

1 cup almond slivers
½ cup coconut
grapes
coconut cream
cinnamon

Heat oven to 350 degrees. In 3 different pans, toast oats, nuts, and coconut separately for about 20 minutes. Stir each pan every 5 minutes until lightly browned.

Mix oats, chia/flax meal, cinnamon, salt, and 2 cups of vanilla almond milk in a large bowl. Stir until it is thoroughly mixed. Add remaining milk and stir. This mixture can be saved in the refrigerator and used for up to a week in individual servings.

When ready to serve, place 1 cup of porridge in a bowl. Add 1 tablespoon of nuts, 1 tablespoon of coconut, 5 grapes cut in half, and top with coconut cream and a dash of cinammon.

"Kansas is great and I've enjoyed living in Wichita since moving here from the country. My friends and the people I meet are so grounded and encouraging!" -Charolett Knapic

SHRIMP WELLINGTON WITH CORAL SAUCE

CHEF ADRIAN DELODDER   BELLA VITA BISTRO

2 SERVINGS

6 extra large shrimp with tail on
6 squares puff pastry
½ cup mushrooms, chopped
2 oz onions, finely diced
2 oz chicken stock
pinch of bread crumbs
2 oz white wine
salt and pepper
egg yolk, for brushing

CORAL SAUCE
1 cup heavy cream
2 tbls flour
2 tbls butter
1 tomato, skinned and seeded
salt and pepper to tatse
½ cup shrimp stock
1 oz Cognac (optional)

To make a mushroom paté, in a sauté pan, add olive oil to sauté onions until they are tender and transluscent. Add the mushrooms and mix well. Add white wine. Reduce the wine by half, and add salt and pepper to taste. Add a little water if the mixture is too dry. Finish by adding a touch of bread crumbs. Mushrooms should hold form when pressed together. Let the mushroom paté cool.

To assemble the Wellingtons, add a spoonful of mushroom paté in the middle of a pastry sheet. Next, place butterflied shrimp on mushroom paté. Take all sides of the pastry and press together to form an airtight seal, except for the shrimp tail coming out of the top.

Brush all sides of pastries with egg yolk.

To make the coral sauce, melt butter in a medium saucepan. Add flour and make a roux. Add cream, stock, and tomato, and simmer for 10 minutes. Add salt and pepper to taste. Add Cognac, if desired. Sauce should be a rose red color. Set aside.

Place Wellingtons on a sheet pan and bake for approximately 15 minutes at 450 degrees, or until golden brown on all sides.

Remove Wellingtons from oven and let rest. On a platter, ladle sauce in the middle, forming a circle. Place 3 Wellingtons around sauce. Garnish with fresh dill or herb.

SHRIMP STOCK- add shells of shrimp, chopped carrots, onions, celery, thyme, tomatoes, and water. Boil for 1 hour. Strain.

HARVEY'S AWARD-WINNING REUBEN

CHEF JD HARVEY   THE CANDLE CLUB

*Working at a Kansas City staple Irish pub inspired me to recreate this classic dish.
The success of this recipe is using the best quality corned beef you can find. -JD Harvey*

4 SERVINGS

24 oz corned beef
8 oz sauerkraut
8 slices thick cut rye bread
8 slices Swiss cheese

HARVEY'S REUBEN SAUCE
¼ cup mayonnaise
¼ cup fancy ketchup
¼ cup prepared horseradish
1 tbls sweet pickle relish

Preheat griddle to medium high. Brush one side of every slice of bread liberally with melted butter. Place bread on hot griddle (butter side down), and add one piece of Swiss cheese to each slice. Grill bread until golden brown and cheese has melted. Remove and set aside. Add corned beef and sauerkraut to hot griddle. Be sure to mix the corned beef and sauerkraut evenly. Continue stirring and flipping until mixture is thoroughly heated.

Top 4 pieces of bread with corned beef/sauerkraut mixture and 2 tablespoons of Harvey's Reuben sauce. Stack it high! Top with remaining slice of bread. Cut sandwich in half and serve with your favorite side.

GINTARA SAIKYO-YAKI

CHEF DAVID KANAI   KANAI SUSHI

A traditional Washoku (Japanese cuisine) that I learned from my Japanese Master Chef.
The delicacy of its flavors have been accepted by a majority of customers I served internationally.
When they try the dish, they say, "Oishii!" (Delicious!) -David Kanai

4 SERVINGS

4 Alaskan black cod, 6 oz each*
1 cup saké

SAIKYO MISO
1 pound Japanese white miso
150 ml saké
150 ml mirin (cooking saké)

1 stalk yamagobo (Japanese pickled bwdock root), for garnish

To make Saikyo Miso, mix together saké and mirin in a mixing bowl. Add miso and stir until miso is dissolved.

Pat black cod fillets gently with paper towels. Place fillets in glass tray and marinate them with Saikyo Miso. Cover fillets with enough miso and cover with plastic wrap. Leave in refrigerator for 24 hours.

Preheat oven to 350 degrees. Wipe off miso from fillets and put them in a bowl of saké for 30 seconds. Pat dry and place fillets in oven and grill until fish turns light brown, about 10 minutes. Watch them closely so they do not burn.

Place fillets on platter and garnish with yamagobo.

*Sea Bass may be used as a substitute for black cod.

"I have served Japanese food in Los Angeles and other big cities for over 20 years. Throughout experience, I realized people from Midwest don't have much experience of authentic Japanese food. That is why I came to Wichita, and I want to carry on my mission as a Japanese chef to introduce Japanese food to more people."

-Chef David Kanai

OCEAN ON PRAIRIE

CHEF DAVID KANAI   KANAI SUSHI

Each shellfish is delicate. Just sear the scallop, do not cook them all the way.
Also, do not fry the oyster for too long. The inside should be raw/half cooked. -David Kanai

4 SERVINGS

8 scallops from Hokkaido, Japan
8 Botan shrimp (sweet raw shrimp)
16 Japanese oysters
2 eggs, beaten
1 cup Panko bread crumbs
1 cup flour
cornstarch, for frying
vegetable oil, for frying

KIWI DRESSING
4 kiwis
2 tsp Japanese QP mayo
30 ml honey or maple syrup
20 ml canola oil

To make kiwi dressing, peel skin off of the kiwis and cut them to $1/8$ inch pieces. Place all dressing ingredients into blender. Blend for 45 seconds, or until all ingredients are well mixed. Refrigerate dressing for a few hours.

Sear scallop in a frying pan until it is lightly browned.

Peel skin off of Botan shrimp, but keep tail on. Use cornstarch and fry shrimp head until it gets crispy.

Dip each oyster into flour mixture, then into the egg, and then into panko crumbs to coat. Heat the oil in a deep fryer to 375 degrees. Drop each oyster and fry them for about 1 minute, until it gets crispy and light golden brown.

On a plate, place the scallop, Botan shrimp, and oyster. Garnish with shrimp head in the center and spoon kiwi dressing onto each shellfish.

BOLOGNESE

TY ISSA   YA YA'S EUROBISTRO

8-10 SERVINGS

1 onion, finely diced
2 carrots, peeled and chopped
1/3 bunch of celery, rough chopped
3/4 cup roasted garlic
1/4 cup tomato paste
rosemary, oregano, and thyme, rough chopped to equal 1/3 cup
1- 32 oz. can puréed tomatoes
2 cups red wine
2 pounds ground beef
1 pound ground sausage
1/3 cup cream
2 tbls salt
3/4 tbls pepper
1 pinch chili flakes
2 bay leaves

1 package of spaghetti
arugula, for garnish

In a food processor, chop the carrots, celery, and garlic separately. Heat oil in a sauté pan and add the chopped vegetables along with the onions and the chopped herbs. Sauté until the onions are translucent. Deglaze the pan with red wine. Add the ground beef and sausage and reduce the red wine by half. Add the rest of the ingredients and cook for 1 1/2 hours or until the sauce has thickened.

Cook pasta according to package directions. Drain and mix thoroughly with bolognese sauce. Plate and garnish with arugula.

DESSERTS

STUFFED FIGS   93

CRÈME BRÛLÈE WITH
A STRAWBERRY ROSE   95

GUINNESS STOUT CAKE   96

COTTAGE CHEESE PIE   100

SOUTHERN PECAN PIE   101

CITRUSY LEMON BARS   102

GOAT CHEESE CHEESECAKE   104

COCONUT MACAROONS   105

TATE CAKE   107

STUFFED FIGS

MASTER CHOCOLATIER BETH TULLY   COCOA DOLCE

One glorious fig makes a complete dessert. The very best, extra-fancy, dried figs are in the market from October to March. Look for moist fruit with supple texture and full shape for stuffing. -Beth Tully

24-36 FIGS

1 cup heavy cream
8 oz bittersweet chocolate (52 – 62% cacao), finely chopped
24 to 36 dried Calimyrna figs
1 ½ lbs bittersweet chocolate, tempered

In a saucepan, heat the cream over medium high heat, just until it begins to boil. Remove from the heat and add the finely chopped bittersweet chocolate. Stir until smooth with a rubber spatula. Pour the mixture into a bowl, cover with plastic wrap and let set for 6 to 8 hours at room temperature.

Prepare the figs for stuffing by heating them gently, wrapped in a damp towel on 50% power for about 30 seconds until the fig is soft and pliable.

When the ganache is set, gently stir with a rubber spatula a few times. Spoon into a pastry bag fitted with a round ¼ inch tip (#803). Hold each fig's stem gently between your index and middle fingers, using your thumb to support the plump fruit. You may need to insert a wooden skewer in the bottom of the fig and wiggle it to enlarge the hole slightly for stuffing. Insert the tip of the pastry bag into the fig's bottom. Gently squeeze, stuffing until the fig is plump and full. Do not worry about leaks in the fig's skin. They can be fixed later.

Place filled figs on a parchment or waxed paper-lined pan and allow to set at room temperature for at least 2 hours. Using a sharp knife, scrape the excess filling from each fig's exterior. To dip, follow the tempering instructions. Holding it by the stem, dip the bottom half of each fig in bittersweet chocolate. Place the fruit back on the parchment-lined pan and let chocolate set. Snip off the very tip of each stem, which is too tough to be eaten.

*Tempering Instructions
Chocolate must be carefully tempered (or pre-crystallized to achieve the luster, proper melting properties, and stability of quality chocolates).   Chocolate may be melted in the microwave. The cooking time will vary with the kind of microwave and the amount of chocolate. Place the chocolate in a microwave-safe plastic container. Chocolate should be broken up; it will melt faster and more evenly in small pieces. Microwave on high for one minute. Stir. Use rubber spatula to coax remaining soft pieces to melt. Continue to stir and if necessary, continue microwaving in 5-10 second increments until melting is complete. Chocolate should appear smooth, shiny, and free of bubbles, grainy consistency, or lumps. The melted chocolate is in temper and ready to be used!

Tempering Tips
-Heat SLOWLY! Do not overheat. Even though it seems as if the chocolate is melting too slowly, 5 seconds will make a significant difference!
-White chocolate will melt slower than milk chocolate, dark chocolate the slowest
-Use high quality chocolate for all cooking projects—the better the ingredient, the better the results.

CRÈME BRÛLÉE WITH A STRAWBERRY ROSE

CHEF ADRIAN DELODDER   BELLA VITA BISTRO

6 SERVINGS

6 egg yolks
1 quart heavy cream
1 vanilla bean or 2 oz vanilla extract
1 cup sugar (divided)
2 quarts water
6 fresh, plump strawberries

Preheat oven to 325 degrees.

In a medium sauce pan, add heavy cream and vanilla bean. Steep the vanilla bean in the cream for 15 minutes. In a separate bowl, mix together egg yolks and ½ cup of sugar. Remove the vanilla bean from the cream, and allow to cool slightly. Very slowly, add the cream into the egg and sugar mixture, constantly stirring. Mix until the cream looks like melted butter.

In 6 ramekins, add the cream mixture almost to the top. Take ramekins and place them in a shallow pan. Fill the pan with water halfway up the sides of the ramekins. Bake in preheated oven for 40-45 minutes.

Remove from oven and let cool for 3 hours, or up to 2 days. To finish, sprinkle sugar on top of the cooled brûlées. Lightly torch sugar to brown.

Place strawberry stem side down on a cutting board. With a small knife, cut into all sides and slowly pry down, followed by the next layer. Cut off the tip to reveal strawberry flower. Place next to the prepared brûlée.

GUINNESS STOUT CAKE

MASTER CHOCOLATIER BETH TULLY   COCOA DOLCE

St. Patrick's Day is a huge event in our family. We do Irish stew, Colcannon, Brown bread, and this cake as our traditional meal- served always on the 17th of March. -Beth Tully

12 SERVINGS

2 cups Guinness Stout
2 cups (4 sticks) unsalted butter
1 ½ cups unsweetened cocoa powder (preferably Dutch-process)
4 cups all purpose flour
4 cups sugar
1 tbls baking soda
1 ½ tsp salt
4 large eggs
1 ⅓ cups sour cream

ICING
2 cups whipping cream
1 lb bittersweet (not unsweetened) or semisweet chocolate, chopped

Preheat oven to 350 degrees.

Butter three 8-inch round cake pans with 2-inch high sides. Line with parchment paper. Butter paper. Bring 2 cups of stout and 2 cups of butter to simmer in a heavy, large saucepan over medium heat. Add cocoa powder and whisk until mixture is smooth. Cool slightly.

Whisk flour, sugar, baking soda, and salt in a large bowl. Using an electric mixer, beat eggs and sour cream in a separate bowl to blend. Add the stout-chocolate mixture to the egg mixture and beat just to combine. Add the flour mixture and beat briefly on slow speed. Using a rubber spatuala, fold batter until completely combined. Divide batter equally among prepared pans. Bake the cakes until a tester inserted into center of cakes comes out clean, about 35 minutes. Transfer cakes to rack; cool 10 minutes. Turn cakes out onto rack and cool completely.

To make the icing, bring cream to a simmer in heavy, medium saucepan. Remove from heat. Add chopped chocolate and whisk until melted and smooth. Refrigerate until icing is spreadable, stirring frequently, about 2 hours.

To assemble the cake, place 1 cake layer on plate. Spread ⅔ cup of icing over. Top with second cake layer. Spread ⅔ cup icing over. Top with third cake layer. Spread remaining icing over top and sides of cake.

"Wichita is a great food town with a really diverse and eclectic variety of dining choices. I have always felt that Wichita is the reason Cocoa Dolce has been so successful because Wichitans love new things and have encouraged us to experiment and challenge them." -Beth Tully

COTTAGE CHEESE PIE

JENNIFER RAY   THE MONARCH

My grandma made this pie for us when we were growing up. It reminds me of being a kid with my extended family. Cottage cheese pie was my grandma's answer to leftover clabbered milk that they made on their farm in Ellinwood. -Jennifer Ray

6-8 SERVINGS

2 eggs
1 cup milk
½ cup sugar
1 cup cottage cheese
pie crust

In a mixing bowl, beat eggs. Add milk and sugar. Mix well until sugar is dissolved. Add cottage cheese and pour into prepared pie crust. Bake at 325 degrees for 25 minutes, or until a knife inserted into the center comes out clean.

Cool for one hour before serving. Store any leftovers in the refrigerator.

SOUTHERN PECAN PIE

BRIAN & KENDRA CHOY   WHEN PIGS FLY BBQ

This is simple, homemade baking at it's finest. Make sure to let the pie cool completely before serving, or it won't set properly and will fall apart. -Kendra Choy

6-8 SERVINGS

3 eggs
1 tbls vanilla
¼ cup dark Karo syrup
1 cup sugar
3 tbls melted butter
1 ½ cup pecan halves
pie crust

Beat eggs and vanilla together. Slowly add in melted Karo syrup and melted butter. Whisk until blended well. Mix in sugar and stir in pecans. Pour the mixture into a pie shell. Place the pie shell on cookie sheet and bake at 375 degrees for 10 minutes. After 10 minutes, rotate the pie and lower the oven temperature to 325 degrees. Bake for another 30 minutes, rotating the pie every 15 minutes. Pie will bubble up while baking. The center will have some small cracks and a slight wiggle (jello consistency) when done. Let cool 2 hours before serving.

CITRUSY LEMON BARS

CHEF KELLY RAE LEFFEL, SARAH OSBORN-BENNETT   TANYA'S SOUP KITCHEN

I came up with this version of the lemon bar when Schane Gross asked me to make desserts for The Anchor when it first became a restaurant. Tip: Use freshly sqeezed lemon juice! -Kelly Rae Leffel

12 SERVINGS

CRUST
1 3/4 cups flour
1/4 cup corn starch
3/4 cup powdered sugar
1/4 tsp salt
1/2 lb butter

CUSTARD
4 eggs
1 1/3 cup sugar
1/4 cup flour
1/3 cup milk
1/4 tsp salt
3/4 cup lemon juice
2 lemons, 1 lime, and 1 orange, zested

Preheat oven to 350 degrees.

To make the crust, melt butter and let cool. Mix dry ingredients together. Add the melted butter and stir until it forms into dough. Press dough in a 9 x 13 pan. Cook for 15-20 minutes. Let cool.

For the custard, combine all ingredients. Pour over the crust and bake for 25-30 minutes.

Sprinkle with confectioner's sugar.

GOAT CHEESE CHEESECAKE

CHEF JOHN CONKLIN

One of my signature dishes. This dense yet ever so light cheesecake was 3 years in development.   -John Conklin

2 CHEESECAKES

CRUST
3 cups graham cracker crumbs
3 cups granulated sugar
1 lb unsalted butter

BATTER
3 lbs chevre goat cheese
3 lbs cream cheese
8 large eggs
4 cups granulated sugar
1 ½ tbls vanilla extract
4 large oranges, zested
2 cups heavy cream
2 tsp kosher salt

Preheat oven to 400 degrees.

On low heat, slowly melt the butter, stirring constantly. Remove from heat. While melting the butter, in a food processor, combine graham and sugar and blend on high till a fine, sand-like consistency is achieved. Place in a metal mixing bowl. Add ¾ of the melted butter and thoroughly incorporate the graham mixture with the butter. The consistency should be that of slightly wet sand- holds together when squeezed, but does not overtly sweat butter. Add remainder of butter as needed.

In (2)-9 inch spring form pans, form crust around the bottom and the walls, leaving a ¼ inch rim open at the top. All walls and bottom crust should be ¼ inch thick. On the top rack of your pre-heated oven, place the cheesecake crusts and bake for 10-12 minutes. With a dry hand towel, lightly tamp down every area of the crust, to siphon off excess butter. Refrigerate for at least 30 minutes, but no more than 12 hours.

In an electric mixer on medium speed, whip the eggs. Slowly add sugar until it has a creamy, pale-yellow consistency. Alternating between cheeses, slowly incorporate with eggs and sugar. Add orange zest and vanilla. While mixing, scorch heavy cream in a hot sauce pan. Slowly add heavy cream to cheese base, ¼ cup at a time (you will not use all of it), looking for a medium stiff peak when completely incorporated. Once density is achieved, add 2 teaspoons of kosher salt. Let mix rest, uncovered for 3 hours.

Once the batter has rested, double wrap the outside of spring form pans with tin foil. Set in a baking pan with water ¾ of the way up the pans (use one pan per baking dish). Add cheesecake batter to the rim of the crust. Bake uncovered at 400 degrees for 1.5 hours, or until a toothpick in center comes out clean. Cheesecakes must rest for 6 hours minimum, before cutting and serving.

COCONUT MACAROONS

TONY ABDAYEM   LA GALETTE CAFE & DELI

It's fun working with people, especially in Wichita, because they like to try different things and share the culture of other food. -Tony Abdayem

30 COOKIES

1 ¼ lbs fine coconut
1 tsp vanilla
2 oz melted butter
2 oz flour
2 oz powdered milk
½ lb granulated sugar
½ liter egg whites, beaten to soft peaks
red dry cherries, for decorating

Preheat oven to 350 degrees.

Put the sugar in a cake pan and cover with aluminum foil. Place in the oven for 20 minutes. When warm, remove from oven and transfer to a mixing bowl. Add coconut, vanilla, butter, powdered milk, flour, and egg whites. Mix well, and place dough in a piping bag.

Squeeze dough out of piping bag onto cookie sheets in a 2-3 inch circle. Decorate with red cherry in the middle. Bake for 12 or 15 minutes. Cool on wire rack.

TATE CAKE

CHEF DANA TATE   BOCCO DELI

This recipe was passed on to me from my dear Great Aunt Hazel. This recipe is a family tradition and requested by many. It brings so much happiness to all. Always make it with tons of love! -Dana Tate

12 SERVINGS

2 sticks of butter
4 tbls cocoa
1 cup water
2 cups sugar
2 cups flour
1 tsp baking soda
½ tsp salt
1 tsp cinnamon
2 eggs
½ cup buttermilk
1 tsp vanilla

CHOCOLATE ICING
1 stick butter
3 heaping tbls cocoa
3-4 tbls buttermilk
1 tsp vanilla
16 oz powdered sugar

Preheat oven to 350 degrees.

To make the cake, boil together butter, cocoa and water for 2 minutes.

In another bowl, mix together all dry ingredients. Add butter mixture to dry ingredients and blend lightly. Add eggs, buttermilk and vanilla. Mix well.

Pour cake batter into 11 x 16 greased pan. Bake for 15-20 minutes, or until a toothpick placed in center comes out clean. Let cool on wire baking rack.

To make the chocolate icing, bring butter and cocoa to a full boil, then remove from heat. Add buttermilk and vanilla to the butter-cocoa mixture, and mix in powdered sugar to a frosting consistency. Frost on cooled cake and serve.

"Wichita holds a special place in my heart. I grew up here and always dreamed of having my own restaurant. Now I have the honor of bringing delicious food made with love to the awesome community of Wichita, Kansas. Wichita has so many wonderful locally owned restaurants that offer such dee-lish eats. We are so proud and honored to be a part of that. At Bocco Deli, we pride ourselves on the fact that we make everything from scratch daily. It's definitely a labor of love." -Dana Tate

DRINKS & COCKTAILS

HIBISCUS MINT TWIST   112

WATERMELON MINT COCKTAIL   114

BIG WHISKEY   116

ROSÉ SPARKLER   119

CARROT BOOSTER   123

NARANJA SANGUINA   126

NANTUCKET SLEIGH RIDE   127

AGAVE MULE   128

BIG ISLAND MAI TAI   131

THE BRASS FUNKY   134

HIBISCUS MINT TWIST

REVERIE COFFEE ROASTERS

This is another creative concoction that is very refreshing and uses locally produced tea. -Andrew Gough

1 SERVING

1 oz blackberry syrup
6 oz Hibiscus Twist Iced Tea (Cozy Leaf brand)
5 oz Topo Chico mineral water
1 sprig fresh mint

Brew Hibiscus Twist tea as packaging suggests. Pour 6 ounces of tea into a glass and muddle mint leaves. Add 1 ounce of blackberry syrup and 5 ounces of mineral water. Pour all liquids over ice and top with mint.

WATERMELON MINT COCKTAIL

AUSTIN DUGAN   86 COLD PRESS

I love getting the time to sit down and get my hands dirty with mixology. -Austin Dugan

12 SERVINGS

½ watermelon
1 large bunch of fresh mint
12 oz vodka
ice

Juice half of one watermelon in a juicer. Place a couple of mint leaves in a shaker glass and muddle to activate the oils. Add ice to the shaker glass. Pour 1 ounce of vodka and 6 ounces of watermelon juice into the shaker glass over the ice. Shake and pour into a cocktail glass.

Garnish with a mint sprig.

BIG WHISKEY

REVERIE COFFEE ROASTERS

Our non-alcoholic version of an Old Fashioned. Finding the right kind of cherries makes a big difference in this recipe. We use tart cherries. -Andrew Gough

1 SERVING

1 oz simple syrup
2 drops bitters
1 quarter slice of orange
1 cherry
Topo Chico mineral water
Penny Cold Brew concentrate
orange wedge, for garnish

SIMPLE SYRUP
1 cup sugar
1 cup water
2 tbls fresh squeezed orange juice
2 tbls fresh squeezed lemon juice

In a rocks (6 ounce) glass, pour one ounce of simple syrup. Add two drops of bitters. Muddle the orange and the cherry in the syrup. Fill the glass with ice and add 2 ounces of cold brew concentrate. Top off the glass with mineral water and roll in a shaker. Pour back into the glass, and top with an orange wedge for garnish.

To make the simple syrup, dissolve the sugar into the water. Add orange juice and lemon juice and mix well.

ROSÉ SPARKLER

JIM POULSON   CHESTER'S CHOPHOUSE

This drink screams summer. Light on alcohol content and easy to drink. Whether by the pool, at the lake, or sitting on the patio, this cocktail will do the trick. I would personally recommend making this drink in a larger batch- either by the pitcher or in a large cooler to share with friends. -Jim Poulson

1 SERVING

2 oz rosé wine
½ oz Aperol
½ oz rose vermouth
½ oz Quady Essensia
½ oz hibiscus tea syrup
champagne

orange, for garnish

In a collins glass, add rosé wine, Aperol, vermouth, Essensia, and hibiscus syrup. Top the glass with ice, and fill with champagne float. Garnish with orange twist.

"Drinks always taste better when shared with friends and family."

-Jim Poulson

CARROT BOOSTER

AUSTIN DUGAN   86 COLD PRESS

When washing the carrots, scrub the outer skin. When this is done, there is no bitter taste left after. -Austin Dugan

1 SERVING

4 carrots
2 celery stalks
1 apple
4 sprigs fresh parsley

Wash produce thoroughly. Cut all the produce for easy insertion through a juicer. Send all the produce through a juicer, alternating the produce as it goes through.

Serve.

"Creating something healthy is so important for our city and for our people. It's a movement that you will start to see in the food service and it's only going to get bigger. I'm part of the change and I feel it everyday when I serve customers. I LOVE IT!"

-Austin Dugan

NARANJA SANGUINA

MICHAEL FARHA   DISTRICT TAQUERIA

1 SERVING

3/4 oz Herradura Silver
3/4 oz Solerno blood orange liquor
6-8 oz blood orange juice or orange juice
splash of soda water

Fill shaker with tequila, blood orange liquor and (blood) orange juice. Shake well. Pour over ice in a rocks glass, and top off with a splash of soda water. Garnish the rim with a slice of blood orange.

NANTUCKET SLEIGH RIDE

JIM POULSON   CHESTER'S CHOPHOUSE

6 SERVINGS

½ cup cranberry compote
750 ml prosecco

CRANBERRY COMPOTE (Yields 4 cups)
2 lbs fresh or frozen cranberries
1 ½ cups sugar
2 vanilla beans, halved
1 cinnamon stick
1 cup orange juice
3 lemons, juiced

To prepare the cranberry compote, combine all ingredients in a large saucepan and bring to a slow simmer over medium low heat. Simmer until the berries burst and the mixture is a jammy consistency. Transfer to a container and let cool. Refrigerate the compote to chill completely.

Add a heaping spoonful of chilled compote to the bottom of each champagne flute. Fill each flute with prosecco.

AGAVE MULE

MICHAEL FARHA   DISTRICT TAQUERIA

1 SERVING

1 oz 1800 Silver
½ oz agave nectar
6-8 oz ginger beer
½ lime, juiced

Fill a copper mug with ice. Pour in measured amounts of tequila, agave nectar, and fresh squeezed lime. Add ginger beer to the top of the mug. Stir well, and garnish with lime quarters.

BIG ISLAND MAI TAI

ROBERT E. MALICOAT   CHESTER'S CHOPHOUSE

Reminds me of sitting at Kauna Oa Bay watching the sunset and listening to my favoite slack key guitar songs. This cocktail is best consumed with true Hawaiian music in the background whilst wearing your favorite Aloha shirt and shorts with comfortable slippahs on your feet. - Robert Malicoat

1 SERVING

1 ½ oz Bacardi original rum
1 oz Orgeat hazelnut syrup
2 oz orange juice
2 oz pineapple juice
1 oz Myer's dark rum

orange slice, for garnish
cherry, for garnish

Fill a collins glass with ice cubes. Pour Orgeat, rum, orange juice, and pineapple juice over the ice. Float dark rum on top.

Top with a fresh orange slice and cherry, or a pineapple wedge.

"I love to eat. That's when friends and family gather together."

-Robert E. Malicoat

THE BRASS FUNKY

ANDY BOYD, IAN CRANE, & NATHAN JACKEL   CENTRAL STANDARD BREWING

*The Standard Issue is our Grisette, and it's inherent tartness works perfectly for the mid-morning cocktail.
We've also substituted fresh grapefruit juice for the orange juice and used this recipe with our Ashland Farmhouse.
Cheers! -Andy Boyd*

MULTIPLE SERVINGS

orange juice
CSB Standard Issue (available at Central Standard Brewing)

Mix together one part orange juice and two parts Standard Issue. Serve in a tulip glass.

RESTAURANT LIST

86 COLD PRESS (114, 123)

BADE TRUCK (13, 31)

BEAUTIFUL DAY CAFE (77)

BELLA VITA BISTRO (15, 80, 95)

BOCCO DELI (107)

CANDLE CLUB (33, 81)

CENTRAL STANDARD BREWING (134)

CHESTER'S CHOPHOUSE (23, 27, 36, 46, 47, 119, 127, 131)

COCOA DOLCE (93, 96)

COLLEGE HILL DELI (58, 64)

DELANO BBQ (42)

DISTRICT TAQUERIA (66, 126, 128)

DOO-DAH DINER (69)

THE HILL (20)

HOT STONE KOREAN (43, 57)

KANAI SUSHI (82, 86)

KEBABS... (50)

LA GALETTE (65, 105)

MOLINO'S (72)

THE MONARCH (100)

PHO SPECIAL (24)

PUBLIC (38)

REVERIE COFFEE ROASTERS (112, 116)

TANYA'S SOUP KITCHEN (52, 102)

TASTE & SEE (17, 22)

WHEN PIGS FLY BBQ (101)

WINE DIVE (74)

YA YA'S EUROBISTRO (88)

ZAYTUN (63)

"I can't imagine life without a table between us."

That quote hangs in my dining room, and it reflects my heart for fellowship and community. There's nothing I love more than lingering over a meal with my family and friends. Stories about the day, memories, laughter, and conversations about dreams often take place around a table decorated with crumbs, wadded napkins, and rings of condensation from the glasses left on the table.

The image to the left is a photo of my great-grandmother and great-grandfather. I never had the opportunity to meet them, but my mother and my aunts tell me that Grandma Dahlberg hosted Christmas dinners and family gatherings at her home in Chicago. Every year, it was a smorgasboard of Swedish meats, cheeses, and homemade cookies.

I can't give credit to the photographer of this image, because I do not know who captured it. Still, it is one of my favorite photos. To me, the photo defines hospitality and gives a smiling invitation to enjoy the company of family and friends over a hearty meal. Surely everyone who was present at that table was filled that day. Not only with delicious food, but also filled in their souls, because love and community is what we were created for.

I'm no one of any authority to give advice. But one thing I'd like to remind myself and urge to others is to be intentional in relationships. Take time to give, share, and be hospitable to those around you. I'd pay a lofty price to be able to go back in time and experience a seat at the table pictured in this photo. I cannot, but I can make an effort to offer a congenial presence today and in the future, whether I'm sitting around a dining table or not. I hope that you'll find yourself inspired to do the same.

-Jenny Myers

ACKNOWLEDGEMENTS

Cover Design by Leslie Garrelts
Thanks for your input, expertise, and time to help your little sister out!

Design Assistance - Amber Travis
I appreciate your talented eye for design and your positivity not only in this book but also in my life.

Editing Assistance - Amy Williams and Joanne Mehler
My deep gratitude to both of you.

JENNY MYERS

is a wedding and portrait photographer in
Wichita, Kansas. She is fond of black and white images, and
her favorite thing to photograph is laughter.
A wife, and mom to 3 beautiful girls,
she and her husband, Matt, enjoy Saturday night dates and
eating delicious food at local Wichita restaurants.
Her most common food craving is a burger and fries.

www.jennymyersphoto.com